Legends of Krakow

Retold by Anna Majorczyk

Translated by Robin Gill

Illustrated by Katarzyna Borzęcka

WYDAWNICTWO BONA

Original Polish title: *Legendy krakowskie*

Author of legend texts: Anna Majorczyk
Historical consultant: Ewa Rudnicka
Translation: Robin Gill
Proofreading: Christopher M. Peterson
Illustrations and cover illustration: Katarzyna Borzęcka
Layout and preparing covers for print: Monika Stojek
Typographic design and typesetting: Monika Stojek
Editing maps: Monika Stojek

Edition I
ISBN 978-83-62836-31-4

Wydawnictwo Bona sp. z o.o.
ul. Kanonicza 11
31-002 Kraków
Tel. 12 430-22-90
biuro@wydawnictwobona.pl
www.wydawnictwobona.pl
online shop: www.bonamedia.pl

Printing and binding: Drukarnia Stabil

Of Krak,
brave Skuba,
and the Wawel Dragon

According to mediaeval stories, the founder of Krakow was the pagan ruler Krak. He built a fortified castle on Wawel Hill, which gave rise to the city named after that ruler. After Krak's death, the throne was taken up by his daughter, the beautiful Wanda. When she refused the hand of the Germanic Prince Rydygier, he sought to invade Krakow's lands with his armies. To prevent the battle and appease the pagan gods, Wanda jumped into the river, offering her own life. In this way, she saved the city from inevitable destruction, and near the spot where the Vistula laid her body on its bank, her grateful subjects built a mound which survives to this day and is called Wanda's Mound.

Cracovians also tell a slightly different version of the legend of the founder of Krakow and the beginnings of the city. In this tale, the Wawel Dragon plays a major role.

Krak was a good, wise, and prudent ruler. Peace, prosperity, and freedom reigned in his country. Sadly, one day in Wawel's grotto, an uninvited guest arrived—a formidable giant dragon. Its body was covered with scales, flame poured from its jaws, and when it hit the ground with its powerful tail, the castle palisades shook. With time, the monster became more and more insolent: it laid waste to the countryside, kindled fires, and its greed knew no bounds. Sheep and even cows were eaten in a single bite of its jaws. Soon after, it began to kidnap young girls. It is terrible to think what happened to them thereafter! Terror prevailed in the town and nearby villages; the everyday bustle was not to be heard;

everyone hid in their huts and their abandoned fields became overgrown with weeds.

Krak called together his warriors and subjects. They consulted for a long time, but to no avail. Nor was there any daredevil who would dare to face the dragon. Finally, Krak had to announce that he who beat the beast would receive his only daughter Wanda's hand in marriage and would sit on the throne at Wawel.

Days passed, long and dreary, but nobody wanted the difficult task. Finally, before Krak stood a young man, Skuba the cobbler. They talked long, and in vain courtiers pressed their ears against the closed doors of the chamber to overhear whatever they were able. After finishing the meeting, Krak ordered that Skuba be adhered to in everything, even if the young man's requests seemed strange and incomprehensible. Indeed, Skuba did not ask either for a sword, or armour, or a shield, but... for a tanned sheepskin and a bag of sulphur. The cobbler deftly sewed the skin, filled it with sulphur, and made shapely legs with hooves and a tail, not to mention twisted horns. Even the eyes of beads were as they should be. The ram seemed alive. Skuba threw the "animal" over his shoulder and, as night fell, crept into the cave mouth and left it by the entrance.

In the morning, the dragon devoured the "sheep" whole, and then the sulphur began to burn him alive, from the inside out. To quench his thirst, the dragon began to greedily drink the water from the Vistula. He drank and drank, but it brought no relief. The dragon's stomach was getting bigger and bigger, rounder and rounder, from the water, until finally the monster burst like a balloon, disintegrating into a thousand pieces.

Skuba carefully gathered up the pieces of the dragon's skin and then sewed magnificent green shoes for Wanda.

Joy reigned at Wawel, all breathed a sigh of relief, life returned to its old ways, and the city expanded and became wealthier. The brave cobbler married the beautiful Wanda, of course, and sat with her on the Wawel throne. They ruled long and happily, wisely and in harmony, though peddlers in the Market Square claimed that it was Wanda who decided everything, because Skuba, although he disposed of the dragon so cleverly, always listened to his wife's counsel.

Many centuries later, a new dragon appeared before the Dragon's Lair. Although it breathes fire like the monster of legend, none are afraid of it. This cast bronze likeness of the Wawel Dragon, erected by Krakow to commemorate those past events, is especially loved by children.

Of Krak's Mound and Rękawka

Krzemionki Podgórskie is made up of rolling hills of white Jurassic limestone, which is separated from Wawel by the meandering Vistula. Legend has it that in this place, on Lasota Hill, the founder of the city, Duke Krak, was laid to rest in a conical mound raised in his honour which exists to this day. Podgórze, once a former Royal Free Town and now a district of Krakow, keeps the memory of the former ruler alive in legend and the feast day called Rękawka ("sleeve" in Polish), held annually on the Tuesday after Easter.

When the wise and good ruler, Krak, died, throughout his country grief and great sorrow reigned. According to ancient custom, whose guardian was the duke himself, it was decided to honour his memory by raising a permanent, eternal, and imperishable mound. The lofty hills which overlooked Wawel Castle, the Vistula, and the surrounding area were chosen as the grave site.

First, a massive stake was driven into the ground strengthened with stones. Fastened to this were radiating wooden fences, so cleverly constructed that for centuries they could keep the powerful mass of earth in check, so that neither wind nor rain nor the scorching sun could destroy the mound. Then, anyone who was healthy and had even a little strength carried earth up the hill, in clay pots, in wooden pails, but most simply in their sleeves. Some still argue to this day, against the proofs of etymologists, that it was from these sleeves full of earth that the later name of the festival of Rękawka.

And it was not just earth that was carried. Many threw a coin, a spearhead, a bronze belt buckle, or a bead or a ring. With each day the mound grew bigger. When it was finished, a sacred oak tree was planted on its peak. Now a great feast could be arranged, without which the farewell to the deceased would not be appropriate. Krak was remembered with a light heart and without sorrow; by day, there was amusement, and in the evening campfires were lit. Neither food nor drink was wanting.

Every year since then, on the day of the vernal equinox, people met at the foot of the mound to honour the memory of Krak and other dead. The years passed, and in the land of Krakow Christianity prevailed. The sacred oak tree was cut down so that it did not recall the pagan custom and old beliefs. Despite this, the Rękawka tradition has survived. Every year on the first Tuesday after Easter, Cracovians came to the mound to have fun and feast. The wealthier townspeople climbed to the top of the mound, again with full sleeves. They were not filled with earth, though, but fruits, kolaches, bagels, sweets, and small change. These were scattered, and the children, students, and those who did not always have enough for such luxuries caught them amid general mirth and pushing.

In 1784, the Emperor Joseph II bestowed city rights on Podgórze. In the mid-nineteenth century, during the reign of Emperor Franz Joseph, Krak's Mound was fortified as part of the construction of Fortress Krakow. Rękawka then moved to the front of Church of St. Benedict, but soon after merriment and spreading gifts were banned. From then on, bagels and sweets could be bought at fair stalls, which are still traditionally set up here to this day.

In the early twenty-first century, the tradition of celebrating Rękawka at the foot of Krak's Mound was revived: during the historical reconstruction the sacred fire is kindled, Slavic warriors engage in single combat, and ancient ceremonies and crafts are presented.

Of Lajkonik

Zwierzyniec is one of Krakow's most beautiful districts. Here the green Błonia extends, a huge meadow in the city centre. At its opposite edges are two newly renovated football stadiums for the Krakow clubs: Cracovia and Wisła. On St. Bronisława's Hill stands the Romanesque Church of the Holy Saviour and a mound raised in 1820-1823 in honour of General Tadeusz Kościuszko, later fortified by the Emperor Franz Joseph I. Above the Vistula, defensive walls rise surrounding the church and convent of the Norbertine Sisters, who farmed in Zwierzyniec as far back as the Middle Ages. Every Easter Monday there is a holiday fair here called Emmaus, and on the first Thursday following Corpus Christi a colourful and cheerful procession leaves the monastery courtyard for Krakow. Among the colourfully dressed musicians, a strange figure in a Turkish jacket and a red robe, with a tall, richly decorated turban on his head, prances on a wooden horse. This is Lajkonik. And legend tells whence he came to Zwierzyniec.

This story took place in 1287, during the reign of Leszek the Black. At that time, Zwierzyniec was a settlement outside the city walls where city farmers and masons lived, but above all rafters. Their task was to sail the Vistula with heavy tree trunks from the royal forests. The rafter not only had to know the river and its whims perfectly, but had to be strong as an ox, as courageous as a bear, and ready at every moment to assist his comrades.

That day, as every year, the solemn Corpus Christi procession was held in Krakow. The procession included the duke himself, knights, and the lords and burghers of Krakow. Then the city guards began to sound the alarm and call upon the inhabitants for defence because they saw the Tartars approaching the city from Zwierzyniec. Terror fell upon them all. Twice already the warriors from the east had attacked the city, burning houses, plundering, and taking men, women, and children into captivity, cruel bondage from which they usually never returned. Was it to be repeated a third time? Soon, at the behest of the duke, all the city gates were closed for safety, and the defenders assembled on the walls watched in horror as the Tartars swarmed like locusts towards Krakow. The first to fall would be Zwierzyniec and its inhabitants...

They did not, however, appreciate the brave Zwierzyniec rafters. In the face of imminent disaster, the raftsmen kept a cool head, reached for their weapons, and near the Norbertine Convent stood to fight the Tartars, who expected no resistance and were certain of easy booty. The balance of victory tilted to one side, then the other, bodies fell in piles, but each dead rafter was immediately replaced by another two, ready to fight to the last drop of blood. When it seemed that, despite their heroic defence, the better-armed and more-seasoned Tartars would win, their commander drove too far into the ranks of the Zwierzyniec defenders. These immediately surrounded the Khan, and one of rafters wounded him mortally. Deprived of his command, the Tartars began to retreat, until at last they fled in confusion.

The heroic defenders, raising cries of joy, moved to Krakow in a merry procession. At its head, on a trophy horse, rode the raftsman who had defeated the Khan, dressed in his rich robes. In the Main Market Square, the defenders paid homage to the duke, who in turn generously rewarded their merits and with the best brew from his cellars raised a toast to the health and welfare of the rafters.

In memory of the brave deeds of the Zwierzyniec rafters, each year, in the octave of Corpus Christi, a joyous procession moves from the courtyard of the Norbertine Convent to the Main Market Square. At its head marches Lajkonik, in stylised Oriental garb. He is accompanied by a procession of raftsmen and the Mlaskot folk band, playing on drums, violins, and basses. Lajkonik visits shops and market stalls whose owners have to pay symbolic tribute to him, and he in return gently strikes them with a symbolic mace to provide them with health and prosperity. The procession covers the same route as the erstwhile defenders of Zwierzyniec. In the Main Market Square he is greeted by the mayor, and together with Lajkonik drinks a goblet of vintage wine. Then, until evening, Lajkonik prances around the Market Square and performs a symbolic dance with a banner, using his mace for "good fortune", and no one avoids it as it is well known that anyone who is touched by Lajkonik will have a good year, and the ladies will surely find their beloved.

Of Krakow's pigeons

Krakow's Main Market Square, one of the largest market squares in Europe, was marked out after the city was vested with Magdeburg rights by Duke Boleslaw the Chaste in 1257. The expansive square is surrounded by historic buildings, and at its centre, in the Cloth Hall, trade is king, as it has been for centuries. The Market Square holds the traditional florist's stalls and the monument to the poet Adam Mickiewicz, affectionately called Adaś. There is also a tower, the remains of the old town hall, where two stone lions stand guard, and the mediaeval churches of St. Adalbert and St. Mary.

The Market Square is also the favourite square of Krakow's pigeons, which city residents have special sympathy for, showing great tolerance for the birds' rather unsanitary habits. This is because they believe that the pigeons are enchanted and came to Krakow because of Duke Henry IV Probus of Wroclaw, when he briefly sat on the Krakow throne (1288-1290).

From the time of the execution of the will of Duke Boleslaw the Wry-mouthed (1138), Krakow enjoyed a special privilege. Namely, it was the capital of the seniorate—the oldest and most important ruler of the Piast dynasty, who had authority over the other regional dukes.

Duke Henry IV was called the Righteous, or from the Latin, Probus, and was ambitious and favoured by fortune. In his home of Wroclaw he ruled, to be sure, with a strong hand, but fairly. Reigning in Silesia, however, was not enough to him; he dreamed of the Krakow throne and being crowned ruler of a united kingdom. When the Krakow High Duke Leszek the Black died, Henry went with his best knights to Krakow to prove by deeds of weaponry that he was worthy of the title of King.

He won the city and now only needed money to beg permission from the Pope in Rome for a coronation. Unfortunately, after the war effort, the treasury was empty. The citizens of Krakow, for whom the new duke was not to their taste, suggested that he ask for counsel from the powerful witch, Marcjanna, because they knew well how evil and dangerous her magic was.

The desperate Henry went to the witch's hut on the Vistula, near Zwierzyniec, under cover of night. The road led the duke across the Błonia, which at that time was not at all a green meadow, but a marshy swamp. A white and deceptive mist always hung there, woven by the witch's spells, in which it was easy to lose your way. But Henry bravely ventured into the labyrinth of winding paths. Marcjanna the Witch already knew that the duke had a courageous and haughty heart, and would stop at nothing. She proposed a contract to him: if he would give her his best knights, she in return would give him as much gold as he desired. Henry became thoughtful, and began to ponder what he might gain and what he might lose. The lust for power was, however, stronger than reason. He agreed. He returned to Wawel Castle and kept watch all night, sometimes sinking into restless slumber; in his sleep he heard the flutter of birds' wings and the sounds of battle.

In the morning he was not greeted by his faithful squire, he did not hear the trumpet playing the morning reveille nor see his knights gathered in the castle courtyard. All the windows and the trees were instead infested with pigeons, with snow-white, black, rusty, brown, and grey feathers. After a while, the birds spread their wings and flew away. Soon after, the citizens saw that huge flocks of pigeons, not seen in the city before, settled on Krakow's houses of worship, the walls of the churches of St. Andrew and St. Adalbert, and the barely-started towers of St. Mary's. It was a strange sight, and many sensed some evil spell in it. And indeed, at one moment, as if on command, the birds took to flight and, with stones in their beaks, soared towards Wawel. Here, right at the feet of the astonished Duke Henry, they dropped their gifts, and every stone, as it fell, turned into pure gold. Then the duke understood how much harm he had caused his honour and his faithful knights, whom Marcjanna had turned into pigeons.

In vain, however, did he search for the witch in her hut on the Vistula River; she had disappeared without a trace. What was Duke Henry to do without his faithful army, alone in Krakow? He collected the gold, packed it in bags and headed for Rome, hoping for papal consent to his coronation, and that prayer would help fix his error. However, he never arrived at the city on the Tiber.

Krakow inhabitants, glad that they got rid of the unwanted ruler, still maintain that it was not Henry's premature death by the hand of a poisoner that upset his coronation plans, but the riotous and unworthy life of the duke who had squandered his magic gold on banquets, games, and tournaments. And Henry Probus' faithful knights, cursed as pigeons, are still waiting for their duke, seeking him in every passer-by, hoping that he has returned to Krakow to free them from their evil spell.

Of the two towers
of St. Mary's Church

*The Basilica of the Assumption of the Blessed Virgin Mary,
standing in the eastern corner of the Main Market Square,
is one of the most impressive churches in Krakow. This
parish church was founded by Bishop Iwo Odrowąż in the
years 1221-1222. It owes its present shape to the extensions
carried out from the 14th to the 16th century. In the years
1477-1489 its most valuable treasure was created – the
main altar carved by Meister Veit Stoss, funded by Krakow burghers. The façade of St. Mary's Church is decorated with two towers: the higher, northern one (81 m),
from which every hour the hejnał bugle call is played by a
bugler, and the lower, southern one (69 m), with five bells.
The disparity between the two towers is explained by a
legend which, though born only in the 19th century, has
permanently entered the tales of old Krakow.*

The citizens of Krakow, contrary to the usual com-
ments about their excessive thriftiness, did not spare
a penny to build their parish house of worship. They
wanted to erect a church worthy of the Blessed Virgin,
which would spread the name of this rich and pious city
around the world. Construction of the planned twin
towers of the church was entrusted to two brothers,
skilled in the art of stone. At first the brothers tried to
work in agreement, but it soon became apparent that
what was moving the work forward was the desire for
fame and competition. Each wished to prove that he was
the better builder, and would erect the more beautiful
tower reaching to the heavens. They decided to work
separately. In the end, they decided that the elder would

build the south tower, and the younger the north. The townspeople were happy with the progress—the towers now climbed as fast as ever.

No one knew how much jealousy was hidden in this job. The brothers looked at each other suspiciously, trying to guess each other's intentions. It soon became apparent that the older, more experienced, was doing better: his building grew more beautiful and more robust. It was also higher. The younger brother could not bear the thought of defeat. He tried to emulate his brother, but soon realised that he would never succeed. Then dark and evil thoughts began to creep into his heart, and as his mind became poisoned, his criminal intention was fulfilled. One evening, the younger brother lured the older to the shores of the Vistula, and stabbed him with a knife. He threw the corpse into the river.

The killer returned to work, but it was nothing like before. He finished building his tower, which, slim and slender, surpassed the unfinished work of his brother. Neither that, however, nor the admiration, congratulations, and cheers of delight, gave him the expected pleasure. He was still haunted by the terrible memory of his brother dying by his hand. Torn by guilt, he climbed his tower, his work paid for in blood, stood on the ledge, and, making sure that the eyes of the townspeople were turned on him and that he would be heard, he confessed his guilt, and stabbed himself with the same knife which he had used to slay his brother. The limp body slumped and fell to the Krakow paving. And the knife, as a warning to future generations and a reminder of the act, which the brothers' false pride and envy had brought upon them, was suspended in the Cloth Hall gate, opposite St. Mary's Church.

❖

Of the hejnal of St. Mary's

The St. Mary's hejnał bugle call is one of the symbols of Krakow. In ancient times, the city guard played the bugle call twice, morning and evening, giving the signal to open and close gates. Apart from that, it was trumpeted as an alarm in an emergency. Today, the hejnał is sounded every hour, and Polish Radio 1 transmits it every day at noon. In the windows of the higher of the two St. Mary's towers, known as the Guard or Bugle Tower, you can see the shining trumpet and the figure of the bugler, who turns to the four corners of the world: in a southerly direction, towards Wawel—in the tradition of playing for the king; to the west, towards the town hall—for the city authorities; to the north, towards the Florian Gate—for visitors; and finally to the east, towards the Small Market Square—in honour of the merchants and fire brigade. The hejnał was played by Polish troops on 18 May 1944 to commemorate the victorious and bloody battle of Monte Cassino. On 11 June 2000, two thousand trumpeters set the Guinness World Record, jointly playing the hejnał in the Main Market Square.

Anyone who hears the hejnał in Krakow's Main Market Square can receive a certificate stating that they have heard it and purchase a commemorative coin in a nearby stall. And if you would like to know why the hejnał stops mid-note, then listen to the legend.

When the Tartar troops once again overran Poland, in Krakow the enemy army was awaited at the gates of the city with trepidation. So every day, around the clock, the guard in St. Mary's tower looked out for the enemy to warn the people in time. The whole city was still asleep when the figures of Tartar warriors began to emerge from the morning fog on the horizon, creeping towards Krakow's walls to attack Krak's town by surprise. The guard, however, remained vigilant. He spotted the enemy and began to sound the alarm, bringing the entire city out of slumber. The defenders immediately reached for their swords and went out to the walls, and the Tartars, enraged that their plan had failed, showered them with a hail of arrows, aiming in particular at the brave guard who, disregarding the danger, relentlessly trumpeted the hejnał to infuse courage in the hearts of Cracovians and cheer them into battle. One of the Tartar's shots hit its target, piercing the bugler's neck, and the melody broke off mid-note. In memory of the brave guard who, according to legend, saved the city, the bugle call still breaks off in mid-beat.

An interesting supplement to the tale of the interrupted hejnał is the story told by Ksawery Pruszyński in the tale *Trębacz z Samarkandy* [The Trumpeter of Samarkand]. During the Second World War, the Polish Army formed under the command of General Anders in the Soviet Union, consisting of amnestied prisoners of the Soviets, and it was stationed in Samarkand in Uzbekistan. The local elders sent a surprising message to the General: they asked that the military buglers play the melody which they had for centuries played from a high tower in the capital of their country. The soldiers guessed they meant the St. Mary's hejnał. They played the hejnał, but asked in curiosity about the reason for this interest. The Samarkand residents explained that it was connected with a former military expedition, which their ancestors, the Tartars, had taken, which ended with a great defeat. In the oral tradition among the people of Samarkand, the conviction survived that that defeat was the result of

God's wrath and a curse for attacking the city when the sound of the trumpets was calling the people to prayer. This curse was borne by the nation until a warrior arrived from the country they had once attacked and played the same tune in the market square, next to the mosque in Samarkand. Whether this is true or literary fiction, it is hard to say. But in every legend there usually lies a grain of truth.

Of the devil's treasure
hidden in Krzysztofory

The magnificent building at the corner of the Main Market Square and Szczepańska Street is the Krzysztofory Palace. This name comes from the statue of St. Christopher (in Polish "Krzysztof") adorning the façade of one of the old gothic houses which was combined and expanded in the 17th century to form today's building. For centuries, the palace often changed owners, many crowned heads visited it, and during the First World War it was a recruitment office for the Polish Legions. Since 1965, Krzysztofory has hosted a branch of the Krakow History Museum, where, among other attractions, you can see the famous Krakow "szopkas" (nativity scenes). From 1961–1980, the mediaeval cellars of the palace, where the Krzysztofory Gallery operated, was the site of the Cricot 2 theatre, established and led by Tadeusz Kantor.

Legend tells of a not necessarily popular tenant of the palace cellars, who was thought to be, and apparently still is, the devil Boruta.

Boruta is one of the most cunning and malicious devils in Poland, and also one of the richest. He usually lived in Łęczyca, an old castle on the Bzura River, but he also liked to look into Krakow from time to time. Today he comes to town less and less; too much has changed here. The regulated rivers—the Vistula, Rudawa, and Wilga— no longer flood every spring, the backwaters and old marshes, which—in addition to cellars—were Boruta's favourite lair, have disappeared around the city.

Long ago, cellars were as they should be: vast, deep, dark, and damp. The cellars under Krzysztofory were particularly impressive. Their winding corridors led as far as St. Mary's Church, and some said that it was possible to journey as far as Wawel.

The Krzysztofory dungeons pleased Boruta, and he kept some of his vast treasure here. It was a good hiding place, because no one dared to venture beyond the boundaries of the storeroom, where equal rows of wooden shelves held Hungarian wine and hoppy beer, and where first class meads were laid down in the basement chill. Boruta valued the area because he liked fine spirits, and his head was strong so he often treated himself to this and that. Many of the palace servants who went down to the cellars happened to see a noble character in a four-cornered cap nosing around the shelves in the flickering torchlight. This figure, however, quickly dissolved into the darkness. Only a strange chill and the smell of sulphur wafted through the basement. He who was wise knew at once that it was an unclean force, and quickly fled the dungeon.

In the end, only the cook Ludwisia was not afraid to go down there. She spat over her left shoulder to remove the charm, and laughed at all the fears. Boruta was displeased with this, because his devil's pride could not bear such apparent disdain. He thought long and hard about how to punish the impertinent cook. One day, Ludwisia, whistling merrily, went down to the cellar, where she saw a huge black rooster who stared at her with glowing red eyes. She knew at once that the devil had changed his form to make her squirm with some kind of joke.

"I have you, you rascal!" she cried out. "You'll be soup before you know it!"

And she ran towards the rooster to grab it. The surprised devil hopped towards the secret door which parted wide before him, and behind him leapt Ludwisia.

Boruta led her on a merry chase through his underground corridors, but the tenacious woman did not miss a step.

In a chamber full of treasures from which the glow beat so hard that it hurt the eyes, the rooster disappeared and in its place stood a devil clad in a noble robe and scratching his horns, who exclaimed impatiently, "Take as much gold as you wish, but now leave me alone! Go back upstairs, do not say anything to anyone, and do not look back."

Ludwisia gathered the gold in her apron, smiled to herself, and set off back. When she was almost out, she felt she had been victorious in her skirmish with the devil and ... unable to withstand temptation, glanced behind. She heard the devil's laughter and the secret door began to close. Ludwisia ran as fast as she could, and, barely in time, sped through the gate, which shut with a bang, cutting off her heel. There was a crash, thunder, the earth trembled, the Market Square shook, and Krzysztofory swayed.

Since then, Boruta has avoided meeting people, but still guards his treasure: many have seen the pair of crimson eyes shining in the darkness of the cellars under the palace.

Of Pan Twardowski

Next to the Main Market Square, at the junction of St. Anne's and Jagiellońska Street, is the Collegium Maius, the first home of the Academy of Krakow, one of the oldest universities in Europe. It was founded in 1364 by King Casimir the Great, and renewed by Władysław Jagiełło from the fortune of his deceased wife, Queen Jadwiga, who bequeathed the Academy all her personal fortune. Many outstanding students remember those walls—this is where the young Nicolaus Copernicus was educated. The museum here today houses many objects that the scientist used to observe the heavens and calculate. In the 15th century, when studying was a privilege reserved exclusively for boys, the young girl Nawojka studied at the Academy disguised as a boy. When she was recognised, she was expelled from the university, but the knowledge she had acquired she then shared with others. The Academy also saw the beginning of the education of one Twardowski, the legendary Polish sorcerer.

Pan Twardowski was a capable, diligent, and persevering student. Many envied his zeal and ability. Soon, however, his studies no longer sufficed for him, because he wanted to explore the secrets of alchemy and black magic. In a cave in Krzemionki he set up his workshop, where he conducted secret experiments, and in the nearby village of Zakrzówek he opened a small school of sorcery. One day, some inattentive students caused an explosion so powerful that a huge, solid rock broke into a thousand pieces, which are called the Twardowski Rocks.

The years passed, and more and more bitterness and disappointment poisoned Twardowski's heart, because despite his best efforts, he had failed to achieve either of his two dreams: he had discovered neither the secret of eternal youth nor the Philosopher's Stone that changed base metal into gold.

One night, a stranger dressed as a nobleman visited the sorcerer's studio in Krzemionki. He introduced himself as Mephistopheles—a devil of the first rank—and he was ready to fulfil Twardowski's every wish. Under one condition: after one year they would meet in Rome and then Mephistopheles would take Twardowski's soul to hell. However, until that time, he would be his faithful servant. Pan Twardowski did not hesitate long and signed a pact with the devil in his own blood.

From then on, Pan Twardowski was famous. Through his magic unguents, he rejuvenated himself and others miraculously. From the devil he received a cock on which he could traverse the entire country in one night. Thanks to spells, he sailed the Vistula against the current without oars. He also learned the secret of the Philosopher's Stone at last, and could change anything he wanted into gold. He had so much of it, that one day he soared over Krakow's Market Square on his cock and threw gold coins down to the inhabitants. As a joke, Twardowski ordered the devil to collect all the silver in Poland and hide it underground near Krakow. Since then, silver has been mined under the town of Olkusz. Twardowski's fame, growing with each day, even reached Wawel and King Sigismund August himself. At his request, the sorcerer summoned the spirit of his beloved deceased queen, Barbara Radziwiłłówna.

The year passed in a flash and Mephistopheles appeared for his due; however, Twardowski had no desire to travel to Rome to give up his soul to the devil, who, like it or not, had to continue serving him. In time, Twardowski became bored with tricks. Instead he began to heal the sick and help the poor—much to the devil's despair. But, as they say, the devil never sleeps.

After seven years of forced service, Mephistopheles decided to pay Twardowski back and came up with a cunning plan. Taking on the form of a servant to some nobleman, he called on Twardowski to help his master, who was apparently dying in an inn near Krakow. Twardowski and the "servant" sat on the cock and in the blink of an eye they were in front of the tavern. When he crossed the threshold, however, he heard diabolical shouts and giggling.

"I have you!" shouted Mephistopheles. "This tavern is called 'Rome', and now you belong to me!"

Having said that, he grabbed Twardowski by the collar and lifted him into the air. Twardowski gazed sadly back at the disappearing Market Square, at Wawel, at his Academy, and, regretting his sinful life, he began to say the hours, the pious song his mother had taught him during his childhood. The words of the prayer so startled Mephistopheles, that he let go of his victim and flew off to who knows where, while Twardowski fell on the very tip of the moon, which rose over Krakow as a crescent. On a cloudless night, you can see him wandering across the moon, waiting for release.

Of the poor fiddler
and Divine Mercy

Every year, hundreds of thousands of pilgrims visit the Shrine of the Divine Mercy in Krakow's Łagiewniki. Here you can see the tomb of Sister Faustina and the image Jezu, ufam Tobie [*Jesus, I trust in You*], *painted strictly according to the saint's guidelines.*

And yet, Krakow bears witness to an even older image of the Divine Mercy. In the 800-year-old Church of the Holy Saviour in Krakow's Zwierzyniec there hangs a painting created in 1605 by Kacper Kurcz. It depicts Jesus crucified, with a golden crown on his head and a white robe. Christ slides one of his golden shoes from his foot towards a fiddler playing below the cross. This image is an illustration of a legend...

In the olden days, in place of today's painting, the Church of the Holy Saviour had an old crucifix. It was said to have been a gift sent from Moravia for Duke Mieszko, Poland's first Christian ruler. Soon after, large numbers of the faithful started to make pilgrimage to this crucifix, and thanks to their offerings, the figure of Christ was clad in a robe sewn of gold and golden shoes.

Legend says that a certain poor musician used to pray before this crucifix. He possessed little apart from his fiddle, and so he came to praise the Lord as he could—with his music. And truly he could play beautifully! He often became so lost in his playing that he was only finally brought to his senses by the distant sound of the bugle calling for the closure of the city gates. He then stood below the cross and with a halting step went to seek some cover for the night, as he did not have a home of his own.

The Lord Jesus felt pity for the poor fiddler. One day, when everyone had already left the church and only the fiddler played his tunes below the cross, a golden shoe slipped from the figure's foot and landed straight between the feet of the amazed player. He looked around and, not seeing anyone, understood that the Lord Jesus himself had offered him this gift. But the fiddler could not accept it. Poor as a church mouse he may have been, but he was more honest than most, and as there had been no witnesses to the miracle, he could easily have been accused of theft. And so he carefully replaced the shoe on Jesus' foot, bowed, and left the church.

Soon after, a ceremonial indulgence took place in the church. Scores of the faithful came, including those from nearby Krakow. After the mass, when the people had already begun to leave, the church was filled with the sound of the fiddle. It was the poor fiddler, as usual, standing below the crucifix and playing his melodies for the Lord. Suddenly, before the eyes of the gathering, the golden shoe once again slipped from Jesus' foot and fell between the player's legs. Now no-one could doubt that the fiddler had experienced a true miracle. The player was allowed to take the shoe with him, and the news of the miraculous event was passed from mouth to mouth to this day. After many years, the crucifix travelled to Italy, and in its place there appeared the image displaying the scene of the Divine Mercy and the fiddler.

✦

Of the Jewish wedding

Kazimierz, today one of the districts of Krakow, was once a separate town founded in the 14th century by King Casimir the Great. For centuries, it held a mixture of Christian and Jewish cultures. It was here, on the site of the ancient village of Bawół, that Krakow's Jews started to settle at the end of the 15th century, soon joined by hordes of brothers of their faith driven from western kingdoms. And so, in the neighbourhood of the Church of Corpus Christi, synagogues began to be built. Seven of these have survived until the present day, including the Old Synagogue from the fifteenth century, the oldest preserved in Poland.

The tragedy of the Holocaust ended the history of Jewish Kazimierz. The majority of its population died, and the abandoned quarter fell into ruin. In recent years, the situation has begun to improve; the synagogues have been restored, and some of them have returned to the Jewish community, reactivated at the end of the twentieth century. Kazimierz is now the host of many galleries, pubs, cafes, and restaurants. The unique, magical climate of the place and the annual summer Festival of Jewish Culture attract more and more tourists.

On Szeroka Street, in front of the Remuh Synagogue and Cemetery, there is a square. Once it was surrounded by a high wall, while today it is a low fence with a menorah motif, the seven-armed candleholder. According to legend, this is the tomb of Jews who ignored the Divine commandments.

Long ago among the many beautiful girls living in Kazimierz was the poor orphan Chana. She worked hard, was pious, and never complained about her fate. David, the son of the baker, fell in love with her, and asked his father so insistently to let him marry the girl that he eventually consented to organise their wedding. The wedding day was chosen; it was a Friday morning. Chana had nothing to give to her dowry, and so, in accordance with custom, all the members of the district were to give offerings. Kazimierz's Jews, however, were reluctant to bring wedding gifts. Morning passed, and then noon, and the young couple were still waiting for their guests. When they were finally all collected, the sun was tipping towards the west and the Sabbath was approaching, the holy time when all devout Jews prayed in the synagogues.

The wise rabbi from the Remuh synagogue married the couple, but asked all those gathered to remain for the Sabbath prayer. Few, however, listened to his advice. The wedding guests went outside, where they feasted at the lavishly laid tables and made merry to the music. The threats and warnings of the rabbi came to nothing, as did those of other Jews outraged by the breaking of God's commandment forbidding celebration on the Sabbath day. Night fell, candles were lit, and the merriment continued. The rabbi warned the merrymakers one last time against Divine anger, after which he returned to the synagogue with the faithful.

When they left some time later, their eyes were met with a monstrous scene—all the partygoers lay dead on the ground.

The wedding guests were buried in the same place they were found, and the site was surrounded by a wall as an eternal warning against breaking the Divine commandments. Allegedly, sometimes, on the Sabbath night, you can hear the calls of the dead from beneath the ground.

❖

Of the Sigismund Bell at Wawel

Wawel is a site that is particularly associated with the history of the Polish state and nation. It holds the royal castle, which was the seat of Poland's rulers for centuries. The gothic cathedral of St. Stanislaus and St. Wenceslas has one Central Europe's largest necropolises, where eminent Poles and kings rest. There are also many legends linked with Wawel Hill. The oldest of these tell of Krak and the Wawel Dragon; from the times of power and the Commonwealth's "Golden Age" there are tales of the wise royal jester Stańczyk and one of the Wawel heads on the ceiling of the Envoys' Chamber. During the Partitions, legends were created to uplift hearts: of an underground castle existing beneath Wawel Hill, where the spirits of the kings live and decide upon the fate of the homeland. There are also legends born in the 20th century, such as those of the chakram, a mystical and holy stone hidden on Wawel which is a source of powerful energy.

On the north tower of Wawel Cathedral in 1521, the most famous bell in Poland was hung, the Sigismund Bell, named after its sponsor Sigismund the Old of the Jagiełło dynasty. The bell weighs over twelve and a half tonnes, is over two metres in diameter, and is to this day set in motion by hand, by twelve bell-ringers. Of the creation of the Sigismund Bell, known as Poland's beating heart, there is also a legend.

The master bronzesmith, Hans Beham of Nuremberg, knew his craft like no other. He carefully selected the proportions of copper and tin so that the sound of the most powerful bell to ever pass through his hands was pure and sonorous. But he was always dissatisfied. Perhaps it was the magnitude of the commission, or perhaps a feeling based on experience, that did not allow the smith to complete his work.

One day King Sigismund himself came to Master Beham's workshop to see his namesake bell. No one knows why, but the king, steered by a sudden impulse, threw his royal golden ring into the boiling alloy. The court lutenist, the splendid Valentin Bakfark, accompanying the ruler, following his lord's example, pulled the strings from his instrument and also threw them into the alloy. "Sincere gifts, that's what the bell was missing," thought the bronzesmith, and knew that at last he could calmly finish his work. All he had left to do was to decorate the bell's sheath with images of St. Stanislaus and St. Sigismund and the coats of arms, the Eagle of the Kingdom of Poland and the Lithuanian Vytis.

Transporting the colossus to the Sigismund Tower was no small challenge. On a specially converted cart with an oaken base, the Sigismund bell was laboriously hoisted up Wawel Hill, where the king and his wife Bona Sforza, courtiers, and burghers awaited its arrival. It was no less difficult to suspend the gigantic bell in its tower. The first time the bell rang from the cathedral tower known as Sigismund's was 13 July 1521. Its melody rang out from Wawel Hill above all of Krakow, filling the people's hearts with great emotion.

Since then, Sigismund has rung for Poland's health and people's intentions. Its beautiful, powerful chime is heard on the most important state and religious occasions, and it also announces particularly important moments. More than once it has announced sadness and mourning for those who have left this world. A cracked tongue would be a bad omen, thus it is always repaired as fast as possible. And it is said that as long as Sigismund's voice is heard, the country will enjoy prosperity and good fortune.

Today, you can climb the Sigismund tower up a winding staircase to see Poland's most famous bell. And it is absolutely essential to touch its tongue, which—strong and powerful—is fantastically good at granting wishes.

Contents

Legend